Anatomy

Karina Vigil

For my parents,
who have nourished my every step.

CONTENTS

HEAD

The foolish mistress,
Who believes everything she thinks.

I still catch sight of her,
The girl I used to be.

I like to lean into the mirror,
And peel back my scalp,
To reveal the dolls,
Nestled inside me.

There she sits,
The me before me.
I stare at her,
The innocence of her,
The naivety of her,
The dreamer in her.

I remember her so well,
And yet, I can hardly recall,
When I let her go.

— Reflection

The moon knew what it meant to fall in love with the
sun,
But she did it anyway.

So what if we part? She thought,
I'll never forget the days that I shined.

— Year one

I wish I still saw time the way I did as a child in August.

Back then, a summer was enough to change everything you thought you knew about yourself and everyone else.

Time is kinder on children. They don't know what it's like to see days as nothing more than a base, for all the to-dos that make you forget what a summer could be in the first place.

May we remember the long days of being a child.

— A child in August

Gold skin and bright eyes,
Hands that orchestrate thoughts,
Punctuation in the form of a finger.

Weathered feet,
That have moved mountains and borders.

A tongue that is more emotion than explanation,
An ancestry that feels comfortable and awkward on my
lips.

I am all these parts,
And yet,
I aim to find a balance between who I am,
And who I could have been.

— Foundation

I store time in the one who lies next to me as I age.

He is the is,
And the was.
The witness to every layer I have grown, and shed.

A private capsule,
That has known my same touch,
In the before,
And the after.

A reminder of who I was,
And who I am.

Then,
Now,
And onwards.

—— Time keeper

I search for their eyes,
Because I can't find you in yours.
But I can't find you in theirs either.

— Lost

They say the grass is always greener,
The only way to ever know,
Is if I leap from this,
From you.

But,

What if the green I leap for,
Never matches the shade of your smile?

What then?

—— The other side

We met in an empty space that we later named us.

We rooted.
I can still recall the feeling of you moving beneath my skin,
Finding path in my pulse.

But,
They watched,
And they waited.
Applying a pressure so fine,
That you exhaled,
And pulled up and away.

I did not fall, but floated,
In all that was robbed.

— Year four

What will happen to the inhale?
Will it stay hanging, afloat?
An unhinged memory, once tethered,
Building a map to steps that we'll never take.
What do they become?
The us,
That was young and hopeful,
Of a forever.

— A final breath before sleep

I found pieces of you.

Tucked in crevasses,
Beneath pits and cheeks,
Between toes and fingers.

Tangled in hair,
Silk and stubble,
Dust and crumbs.

Leftovers.
I nibbled at them,
The sour, stale, sweet mess of them.

I found your kiss,
Tucked in the cracks of my lips,
And I wondered if he felt you when he kissed me.

— After goodbye

If perfect timing had a name it would wear yours proudly.

How convenient,
For your steady strides to find a path,
On the uncertain thoughts that I couldn't keep contained.

Even if my lips never parted with the words of them,
The mighty sky took notice,
And marching in you came.

Heart breaker,
Take your words elsewhere.
You'll never be the one to find rest in the blades of my shoulders.

— A different shade of green

I made a list
And showed it to the sky.
I have yet to receive my reply.

So I stumbled with squinted eyes,
To my next bulleted point.
Try as I might, I can never make out the blurry lines.

I think I may be near sighted.
I am certain that I am back sighted.
Because everything I have passed is in the sharpest relief.

If only the taunting stars would grant me clarity,
For that which I can't see.

— A Plan

Fingers weave to the ballad of affection.

Her head finds rest in the curve of his shoulder,
He takes a moment to marvel at his luck.

Smiles line their downcast eyes.
Mountains dot the outside scenery,
Bowing to their beauty.

I think of you.

— Thoughts on a train in Italy

We are neither here,
Nor there.

A toe in the water of an expansive sea.
We stall on opposing shores,
With a love so deep it mocks the distance between us,
But we don't wade in.

So here we'll stand,
Here we'll grow dry.

— Imperfect timing

Plastic.
What a strange creature we reared.
Flimsy and dull,
Birthed to be discarded for many more days than our own.

One day it will meet that open air,
And forage for branches, sewers and shallow puddles,
Joining colonies of brethren.
A plastic bag is the most common bird of cities after all.

What must the animals think?
I wonder if even dogs marvel at our stupidity.

I know cats do.

— Plastic

The knowledge of the world is stored in the hands of my
father.
He has filled my palms through my ears.

Year after year,
I begin to hear a little more.

Listen,
He says,
You can always begin the song again.

— Papa

I want my parents to know my home.
I want weathered bricks,
And hints of kids scattered on the lawn.
I want curious eyes,
Under dark skies,
Catching a glimpse,
Of all that I am and am not.

— Thoughts on a walk down Sussex

Every now and then,
I feel centred on the unsteady stones laid by my hands.

With not much more than,
A hope,
And a belief,
In the dreamer girl.

With happy hands pressed together,
I'll raise them high to the sky,
Every once in a while,
To marvel at my luck.

— Recognition

HEART

The muscle
The sizzle
The inside of it all.

Take my hand, let us learn to dance with these aching feet.
Light steps now.

— Forward.

We made the setting sun jealous.

The way you made me blush,
Demanded all attention.

It was in the crimson of my cheeks,
That lovers rested their heavy heads.

— First kiss

The moon caught sight of the sun and let out a sigh.

The sigh tickled the water along all the shores,
Until the water had no choice but to surrender to its shape.

Now with every rise and fall, the echo of the sigh can be heard against sand and stone.
This is the moon's love letter to the sun.
A reminder of the moment that took her breath away.

—The birth of waves

All I am is sunshine,
Bright and blind.
I believe they call this bliss.

— Firsts

Bleak winters,
Sticky summer days.

We have grown older but this love does not age.
Youth lies in a feeling unchanged despite repeating
seasons.

In the song that plays and draws your face,
In words said long ago but murmured often.

Time is our guarantee,
As are the sun and the moon.

—   The secret

I discovered late one night,
That our souls sing to each other while we sleep.

— Love language

I know some things, but most things I don't.
I can't tell you why one chemical reacts with another,
Or if there is life beyond our own,
But I know what it feels like to love you,
And sometimes I believe that's enough.

—   Year eight

Can I live here?
Right here, with my head against your shoulder?

I can make my address the nape of your neck,
And grow a garden amongst the hair on your chest.

I need no furniture or walls,
For it is tucked in beside you that I call home.

— Evening routine

My muscles are sore from the weight on my back.
I find relief in your fingers that ease the tender knots I have tied.
How do you do that, how do you give me everything I need without offering anything at all?

—   Lucky

She loved his hands most.

In a world of fists, she unraveled his fingers and found a
place to rest.
With her fingers in his, she felt a comfort often described
but rarely felt.

Words pronounced in feeling,
Thoughts formed by touch,
A realm bridged by fingers.

Her hand in his,
His hand in hers.

—   Hands

We collapsed into each other and built a bridge.
Who knew fingers could reach so far,

In the rubble of our fall we allowed passage,
Offering a chance for uncertain feet to touch foreign soil,
Rich in open heart and solid bones.

I hope their fingers can meet along the way too.

—   An introduction

People throw words at us hoping they'll stick,
But there is no translation for this.
No one has known these words before us,
No one will after.
We are a language all of our own.

—   Almas

Beautiful bird,
If the cage door is open,
Take the leap.

— A departure from fear

When we make it,
Let's throw a party.

We can use the naysayers as streamers,
And build a piñata out of fear.
I'll have you kiss the bat before I swing,
And as the remains rain down as flimsy multi-coloured confetti,
Everyone will cheer.

Once the guests are fed and well drank,
And they've shed happy tears at our journeyed feet,
We will climb into bed,
To hold each other the way we have since the start.

And in the moment before I close my eyes,
I'll hear the ocean,
Or the call of a bird,
Perhaps from here,
Perhaps from there,
And I'll let out a sigh of relief,
The very last one.

—   The end

One day I'll have children.

And they'll know snow capped mountains,
And lush, green leaves.

And I'll know that sweet, sticky, smell of their palms,
The soft texture of their hair beneath my lips.

And when I part for oblivion I will rejoice in the remainder of their lives,
In the fact that I made the right choice in allowing them to be.

— Climate

Parts of me walk independently of my body.
I get to admire these,
rearranged recreations of myself.

Who knew that the same ingredients that built these bones,
Could also reproduce my nose in three different fashions.

Here are my other lives,
At a different age and time.

They are the keys.
Without them,
How would I breathe?

—   Siblings

Dreamer girl.
Faithful to the religion of time,
Have you seen what you've done?
There's a garden in your footprints.
Dear one,
Never forget to admire,
The petals you have grown.

— A love letter to the author by the author

One day you'll take a deep breath,
And find that there is no wish on the other end.
You'll feel the weight of the hands that surround you,
And you'll know it's enough.

— One year older

Steer this ship,
Love what steadies you from above and below,
And when given the choice, adjust the sails.
There is no truth until the end.

—   The risk

LUNGS

The release.

When the small things feel like large things,
I take a deep breath and count.

One,
Two,
Three,
Four steps to stardust.

The same steps that fill my veins,
Make the warm rays that plump house cats take rest in.

Every so often I can feel the ingredients boiling,
Call me a red giant all you want.

A part of it and apart from it,
No wonder I see my mother's eyes in the night sky.

—   Four steps to stardust

What is it that I like anyhow?

I know I like words on paper,
And lemon flavoured desserts.

I know I like the touch of my mother's palm,
And quiet sunsets in the garden of my youth.

I know that I'd like to build steady steps with steady
words,
And I know I'd like to bloom.

I'd like to take the bud nestled deep within,
And will its delicate petals to open.

But there is so little that can rush,
The gentle unfolding of the soul.

Nurtured by time,
And the slow understanding,
Of all the things I know I like,
And all the things I know I don't.

As I grow, I bloom.

—   Bloom

I think I'd like to be a house plant.

Perfectly perched on a sunny sill,
Bathed and nourished,
Pruned and encouraged,
To bloom.

Thinking as much about time,
As time thinks about me.

For that, I would grow leaves.

— The antidote

One day I leaned in close enough,
And discovered that even this circle has an end.

— A new beginning

The clouds outside are purple.
They decorate a thin blue sky searching for night.

Until tomorrow! The sun declares.
And so,
Stoic buildings release a tired breath,
And yawning trees find rest,
And curtains are pulled closed on purple clouds.

Bidding farewell to the very first and last of them.
A one time show,
Eons in the making.
So patient for today,
So ignorant of the promise of tomorrow.

—   Purple clouds

It was in the presence of giants,
That I realized,
Little of the clouds I carry,
Are clouds at all.

For what is fear to the spine of the earth?
I choose to be a mountain,
Eroded by nothing other than time.

—   Trento

It is not lost that my luck,
Was bred from misfortune.
And the destruction of a land,
That gave me everything,
Without knowing me as its own.
Without expecting anything of me in return.

—   Nicaragua

I wish I could sink my arms deep into my mother.

So deep down that I can feel her pulse against my bone.
Until I can recognize it as my own.

Until my arms are mistaken for the trunks of trees,
And birds find a home in the wild growth of me.

Until the roots of my fingers meet her core,
Until I am she and she is me.

Nothing more.

— Mama

Too often I've forgotten the me before me.

There are days that I must remind myself,
That childhood has passed.
Sometimes I feel like I can crawl back into it,
As if it has been on hold,
And at any moment my siblings and I will live as one,
Under the roof of my parents' embrace.

And there are days,
Where I'm certain I'll find myself on the uneven
pavement of my university.
Backpack heavy with books and opportunity.
And after class I'll meet him on the mattress of his
bedroom floor,
Where we'll lie together missing classes and phone calls,
bus times and deadlines,
Everything but each other.

And still —
I wonder when I'll walk back into my best friend's home,
And we will walk side by side,
Dancing to the same song,
Pressing play at the very same time.
Thinking we were above it all,
Only understanding of each other.
And we were.
We are.

So I'm certain,
I'll wait for the day I return to this moment in time too.
When everything has changed from where it currently
stands,

I'll feel as if it is only a long vacation,
From who I was,
And I will once again meet myself,
To relive the glory and beauty of this special kind of life I call my own.

— I hope I don't forget what it's like to be me at this age.

You eat like a girl he says.
I grin,
Showing teeth made strong by meals made to make them
shatter.
Yes, I say, thank you for noticing.

—   Lunch

I am not an ellipsis,
I am the breath between words,
I am the curve of your tongue,
Without me, how would you speak?

—   …

A quiet voice.
A mind that assumes that they are right,
And that I am here among the flowers, aching to rise
above the weeds.

You see, I feed the bees who create thick honey,
A sweetness bred from a thought set free.
An uttered word that quiets a room.
A simple offer laid bare.

I am sweet nectar to be shared.

— Anatomy

There is beauty to her,
In her,
Peel back her skin,
And you'll find fields of flowers.

She welcomes all,
To step foot,
In the magic of her fields.

Plucking the very best parts of her,
And offering it to those,
With poorer soil.

—   A true friend

Clarity struck,
When I shared with you my garden,
And you pointed out the weeds.

— An epiphany

Here I go,
On the verge of collapse,
Into the possibility of one world,
Or the other.
I hope they both have air,
Because I still have not found this breath of mine.
May I find release,
When my toes meet steady ground.

—   The choice

I surrendered to the comfort of the beckoning waves.
At the shore I could reach,
But there was magic in the last touch of sand on my toes,
And stepping into a space never dreamed.

— Apoyo

It was in stillness that I learned why even mountains must
quake.
Movement is the creator,
And I must create.

—   A shift

Exhale,
Until all you're left with is the courageous,
The mountain mover,
the pulse that prevails.
This is what stays dry in a monsoon.

Smothered beneath every doubt ever inhaled,
Behind every victory,
Every considered dream.
Hold —
Feel its weight.

Say hello to everything you thought you lacked.
Rise from the seabed.
You are glory and guts,
You swirl and build,
You explode and create.

— You

Deep breath.
Whatever it is,
The sky will still be blue at the end of it.

— Above the clouds

The moon lights the darkness,
With what little she is given.

— A final reminder

Manufactured by Amazon.ca
Bolton, ON